HOME BUYING ON A BUDGET

Congratulations! I want to first thank you for purchasing my book "Home Buying on a Budget". My purpose for writing this book is to afford everyone the opportunity that I had in life with regards to purchasing a home.

The home buying process, whether it is your first or fifth time, can be not only frightening, but also overwhelming. My goal is to help with one of the most stressful aspects of the home buying process; the money. As a California licensed Realtor, I have seen, time and time again, buyers unable to purchase property simply because they did not have either the down payment, the closing costs, or both.

According to CNBC.com, over 1/3 of people from generations X, Millennial, and Generation Z say that their biggest obstacle in purchasing a home is the down payment. What if I told you that there were programs out there that could afford you a home with no down payment and no closing costs?

My home buying experience has shaped the way in which I operate. What do I mean? Well, I've personally seen my $5,000 investment turn into a net worth of six figures. Purchasing anything that is not going to make me more money in the future is highly discouraged, considering where I want to go in life, as I now understand the value of "making your money work for you," not the other way around.

I look forward to helping you along this path and helping you to understand that buying a home does not have to be as expensive as some make it seem. The majority of the information in this book will be considered material information for first time homebuyers. However, I do believe that someone who has purchased a home before can also gain insight from reading this book.

HOME BUYING ON A BUDGET

Who am I?

I'm a graduate from UC, Santa Barbara with a degree in Business Economics. I moved back home and went from the ultimate party school and endless freedom to living back at home with my mom. To say that it was an adjustment is an understatement. We bickered for the entire time that I lived there. Not only had I gotten used to living on my own and doing what I wanted when I wanted to, my mom for the past four years had done the same.

So simple things like not washing the dishes when she asked, or cleaning the bathroom per her third request caused frictionbetween us. My mom had every right to be upset, though. I was a college graduate who half knew what I wanted to do in life, with a job barely paying over minimum wage. I'll never forget my mom telling me that if I didn't want to follow her rules whilst I lived in her house, I had options; aka "you can move out".

After living in Isla Vista, the 1 mile by 1 mile radius town directly outside of the UCSB campus, where the majority of undergraduates live, for three years, I knew that I never wanted to deal with landlords who harbored slumlord tendencies again.

My mom was the first person who planted in me the seed of purchasing a home; paying my own mortgage instead of paying someone else's. Considering it was 2014 and the housing market had just crashed 6 years earlier, homes were on the market for dirt cheap, but how could I purchase a home? I was just some recent college graduate who was making $37k a year. My mom, an Underwriter with over 25+ years of experience, did the initial research for first time homebuyer programs via good old Google. While helping me prepare to buy, she found the organization HPP Cares.

HPP Cares, short for Home Preservation and Prevention, is an organization that provided first time home buyer seminars which once completed, provided you with a first time home buyers certificate, allowing you to get access to first time home buyers programs across several lenders. The class that they held was an eight-hour Pre-purchase Homebuyer Education Workshop provided only once a quarter. My mom, being the awesome mom that she is, signed me up for the class and had been telling me for weeks about it. Of course, still riding the party wave the ultimate party school trained me to do, I go out partying the night before the class.

HOME BUYING ON A BUDGET

The morning of the class, I honestly was in no state to go and sit in a room for 8 hours and learn anything – I was hung-over. I knew that my mom had done a lot of work to get me signed up and I didn't want to let her down but I was exhausted. After she reminded me that the class was only held once a quarter, I mustered up the little energy that I had in order to get to the class.

Participating in the class required a simple $25 payment along with 25 canned goods, at that time. The course material included anything and everything that you needed to know when it came topurchasing a home. From simple things such as which first time homebuyer programs were available after receiving the certificate once the class was over, to not signing a buyers contract with a realtor until you were sure that you not only wanted to purchase a home, but that you wanted to use that agent. They also explained the home buying process lingo; home inspection, appraisal, down payment, closing costs, etc.

Halfway through the class, during our break, there was a lady I half paid attention to who spoke of a first time homebuyers program through a lender named Boston Private Bank. I, like many people in the room who were not fully educated on this topic, assumed her first time homebuyer program was just like the others we had heard the speaker of the course mention several times just minutes earlier, so I continued to afford this lady very little of my attention.

After leaving the course and receiving the certificate, it was now up to me to choose which program worked best for my circumstances. I was set on using the WISH program from the beginning. The WISH program, which stands for Workforce Initiative Subsidy for Homeownership Program, is a grant program that offers up to $22,000 in grant money that never has to be paid back; provided you do not sell, refinance, transfer title or deed or go into foreclosure for 5 years. The only draw back is that the program does not disperse funds until you are in escrow.

This essentially means that you can go through the entire home buying process; get pre-qualified, find an agent, look for homes, put in an offer, offer get accepted, get into escrow and the program will then let you know if they have the funds available. As you can imagine, that can cause a potential problem if the funds are not

HOME BUYING ON A BUDGET

available once your offer has gotten accepted. I personally did not want to go through the entire home buying process only to be told at the tail end that there were no funds available.

Years later as a realtor, I have represented buyers who had their offer accepted and were unaware of the funds not being available until after the fact. After going through such a long and strenuous process, it hurt me as their agent to see them not get the home because the funding was no longer available. Programs like the WISH program require you to be pre-qualified and ready to purchase a home at all times depending on your seriousness of becoming a homeowner.

What I mean is that as soon as funds become available, you have to hit the ground running, as you are not aware of the amount of funds and how many families are applying until you have an accepted offer on a home. This can take a toll on ones psyche as you have to be resilient; you have to be okay with funds not being available now but knowing that once they do come back, you'll be ready the next time.

Lets go back to the lady earlier from Boston Private Bank that I half paid attention to. I took paperwork from each of the first time homebuyer programs, so after realizing that the WISH program wasn't going to work for me specifically, it was back to the drawing board. I'll never forget my mom calling me while I was at work after she had taken a second glance at the first time homebuyer program provided by Boston Private Bank. She explained to me that they provided an excellent program that was almost too good to be true, so we did our research.

Boston Private Bank offers a Community Homeowner Fixed-Rate Program, which provides specific financing for first-time homebuyers, or those looking to refinance their existing mortgage.

The program hasn't changed much since I used it, but currently, in order to qualify, the property needs to be located in Los Angeles or Ventura County.

HOME BUYING ON A BUDGET

In the program, they offer:

·Fixed-rate mortgage

·Minimum 3% down

·Minimum credit score of 660 on single-family property

·NO Private Mortgage Insurance (PMI)

·Maximum income $95,000; $133,000 if the property is located in a low-or moderate-income census tract.

The property can cost up to the max amount for conforming loan terms.

Let's pause here for a minute to explain a few things; the first being conforming loan amounts. The majority of down payment assistance programs require that a property fall within certain guidelines placed on the loan and/or lending institution by a Government Sponsored Entity (GSE). The two most popular GSE's are Fannie Mae, short for Federal National Mortgage Association (FNMA) and Freddie Mac, short for Federal Home Loan Mortgage Corporation (FHLMC). The conforming loan limit is adjusted every year to reflect the changes in the average price of a home in the U.S.

Fannie Mae and Freddie Mac's federal regulator, Federal Housing Finance Agency (FHFA), uses the October to October percentage increase/decrease in the average house price as indicated in the House Price Index report issued by the Federal Housing Finance Board (FHFB) to adjust the conforming loan limits for the subsequent year.

Basically, the House Price Index report is used to show what the average price of a home in the U.S is. If that number adjusts, the guidelines on how much your loan amount for a residential property is will be adjusted accordingly. Also note that a residential property is defined as a property with 1-4 units, so if you purchase a duplex (2-unit), your conforming loan limits will be adjusted higher and the same if you purchase a 3-unit property and so on.

HOME BUYING ON A BUDGET

Second, let's explain how you find out if a property is within a low to moderate-income census tract. The first step is to visit ffiec.gov – within the page you will see a section titled "Consumer Compliance." Directly below the heading "Consumer Compliance," you will see a link "Geocoding/Mapping System." Click on this link. After clicking on the link, you will find a table labeled "Matched Address" as well as a map directly to the right of that table. In order to find out if a property is located in a low to moderate census tract, you will first want to change the year directly next to the title "FFIEC" to the year prior to the year you are currently in. So if it is 2019, you'll want to change the year to 2018 as census information is not available for the current year.

At the top of the page, put in an address of a property of your interest and press "enter." The map will redirect to the location of the property address that you put into the system and a dropdown will pop up in the top left corner of the map titled "Census Demographic Data". Click on the dropdown and within the table at the top you will see the title "Tract Income Level" under the tab "Census." If the words "low" or "moderate" are displayed directly to the right of the title then this property is within a low or moderate census tract.

Lastly, PMI. Private mortgage insurance protects your lender if you default on the loan in the same fashion that homeowners insurance protects you in case you have problems with your home.
If you are financing your property but do not quite have 20% down,you may be required to pay PMI. In case you default on your mortgage, PMI will pay benefits to your lender to cover the loss. There are two types; mortgage insurance premium or MIP if you decide to get an FHA loan which is government backed, or private mortgage insurance (PMI), if you decide to finance your home through a corporate entity.

Private Mortgage Insurance is required to automatically be canceled once you hit 22% equity or you can request that your lender cancel it at 20% equity. However, with an FHA loan, your mortgage insurance payment is required throughout the lifetime of the loan. You do have the option, though, to start with an FHA mortgage and choose to refinance out of it into a PMI-free mortgage once you have at least 20% equity. Some lenders will not require PMI for certain loan programs even if the borrower has less than 20% down. Consult your

HOME BUYING ON A BUDGET

lender for more details.

Okay let's get back to this unbelievable down payment assistance program at Boston Private Bank. Within this program, they allot up to $15,000 for eligible need-based borrowers with their Equity Builder Program, and the same amount for their Down payment-Closing Cost Assistance Program (D-CAP); the need is based on the income of the borrower. Essentially, the lower your income is, the more money will be provided for the grant.

The income cannot exceed the median income based upon the state and county you live in. Both programs are tacked onto your property as a silent second loan, essentially a lien against the property, and are forgiven after 5 years. This means that if you do not sell, refinance or otherwise transfer ownership of the property within 5 years of the closing date, the loan is forgiven and the lien is removed. Boston Private Bank still uses this exact same program today.

Have no idea what the area median income within your respective state or county is? You can find income qualification information at huduser.gov, and at the top left of the page, click on the dropdown and select "data sets." Under "data sets", you will see the link "income limits" which you will select.

Under the new page, you will find the subheading "Access Individual Income Limits Areas". Click on the link directly below labeled "Click Here for FY IL Documentation." Within this section, you will input the state and county in which you are looking to purchase a home and find the AMI or Area Median Income; you will have to inquire if the program calls for the income limits under very low income (50%), extremely low income (30%) or low income (80%) correlated to family size.

After being spoiled for years in Santa Barbara and never needing a car in order to get around, I saw the value of being able to walk outside my door and go to the grocery store, go to get my nails done, hair, etc. So I set out searching in Long Beach, CA.

Long Beach, CA is a city on the Pacific Coast of the United States located in Los Angeles County. It is the 7thmost populous city in Southern California but is the second largest city in the Los Angeles

HOME BUYING ON A BUDGET

metropolitan area. Long Beach is considered one of the last affordable beach cities in CA. This was not the reason I purchased there, though. What drew me there was the downtown feel on a poor man's budget.

HOME BUYING ON A BUDGET

How did I do it?

So I know you're reading this and thinking, "Well, she purchased a home in 2014 and homes were cheaper then after the housing crash. Homes are expensive now and I don't think that I can afford one." Well, first of all, if you don't believe you can do something, chances are its not going to happen; "Whether you think you can or you can't, you're right" - Henry Ford.

This is one of my favorite quotes of all time because it speaks of your mindset. The very first thing that you have to do when trying to do something is believe that you can do it first. Once you believe it, it will manifest into whatever amount of work you put into getting it done. If you procrastinate, don't plan, don't save money, all of these things will factor into how your home search goes.

As I mentioned earlier, I was a recent college graduate who made $37k a year working as an analyst for a reputable women's fashion company in Los Angeles, living at home with my mom and trying to matriculate through life and figure myself out all along the way.

I had set my mind on purchasing a property and I knew that I couldn't roll in with $0 trying to purchase a home, so saving became my #1 priority. I made a plan for wanting to have $10k in order to be a stronger buyer since I didn't have a lot of money nor a large income amount. So I first figured out what I needed to live off of.

As I told you before, at the time I was living at home with my mom who wasn't charging me any rent, I didn't have a car payment, I had no credit card debt and very minimal student loans. So I calculated what my monthly bills were: food, gas, student loan, utilities, and the occasional drink at a bar. I figured out that I could survive off of $1,000 a month, which meant that I could save the additional $1,000 a month that I received from my monthly salary after taxes.

After six months of saving $1,000, saving my entire tax return and combining that with the little savings that I did have, I got to just under $10,000 saved.

HOME BUYING ON A BUDGET

If you read the above and said to yourself, "I have a ton of credit card debt" and "I'm drowning in thousands of dollars in student loans" along with "Well, I only make $37k now", "I've got horrible credit" and ultimately, "how am I going to be able to afford a home if I don't have the same advantages that she had". If you're saying anything related to the commentary that I just mentioned or any version of that. STOP IT! Remember, buying a home at any stage is hard. I've personally had clients that had $200,000 in the bank with bad credit who had to have a cosigner because of their terrible credit. The most important thing to remember is that if there is a will, there is a way.

HOME BUYING ON A BUDGET

How exactly can YOU do it, though?

Well first of all, the entire reason for me providing such detailed information about me getting the first time homebuyer program was trying to inform you that there is, in fact, money out there that can subsidize your home buying purchase at any level; be it your first time purchasing a home or your third. Let me show you how you can do just that.

If you're looking to find a grant program within your state or county, start by finding homeownership workshops which inform you of available grant programs within your area by going to HUD.gov.

Once on the website page, you want to look for the phrase "What We Do". Once you have identified this at the top of the page, hover over this phrase and when the dropdown appears, click on "Buying a Home". Scroll down and click on the link "Homebuying programs in your state" under "1. Figure out how much you can afford". You will want to click on this link and select the respective state that you live in or plan to purchase residential property in.

After selecting the respective state, scroll down towards the middle of the page under the section "I WANT TO" to find the link "Learn about Homeownership". Within the next page, you will find it titled "Homeownership: (respective state)". So in my case, since I'm based in California, it would say "Homeownership: California". From there, you will see the subtitle "Buying a Home" in which you can click on the link "Assistance programs". The links and information will vary from there based upon the state and county you live in.

It is first important to note that grant and assistance programs are based directly off of where you plan on living. Your best bet is to walk into different lending institutions i.e. a bank within your area or the area you plan on moving, and inquire about what down payment assistance, grant or closing cost assistance programs that they offer.

HOME BUYING ON A BUDGET

Programs Available

NACA:

What is NACA?

NACA, which stands for Neighborhood Assistance Corporation of America, is a non-profit community advocacy and homeownership organization. It is a homebuyer program that allows you to purchase a residential property, anything with 4 units or less, with no money down and no closing costs. Yes you read that correctly. The NACA program allows you to purchase a residential, 1-4 unit property, with no down payment, no closing costs and does not charge PMI; private mortgage insurance. The loan through NACA is a conventional 15yr or 30yr mortgage and does not require perfect credit, high income or savings with interest rates typically lower than the National APR rate. The loan through NACA is a conventional 15yr or 30yr mortgage and does not require perfect credit, high income or savings with interest rates typically lower than the National APR rate. The program offers 100% financing with the well-known lending institution, Bank of America financing your loan.

Who can you qualify for NACA?

Well, you are not required to be a first time homebuyer, however, you cannot own another property at the time of the NACA closing. It is a requirement that the property is owner occupied, so you must live in the property for the duration of the NACA loan. It is a requirement that you are registered to vote except for religious reasons, you must volunteer in 5 activities/actions in a year and must agree to the $25,000 security placed on the home; essentially a lien. The lien is placed on the home for the duration of the NACA loan to ensure that you are not using the home for investment purposes and that the program does in fact help those that truly need it.

What you do have to pay?

With the NACA program, you are required to pay some funds in order to participate. These funds include: property taxes, homeowners insurance, daily interest, inspection and evaluation fees, earnest money deposit, and buy down if applicable.

HOME BUYING ON A BUDGET

NACA is offered in the following states:

• Arizona	• Illinois	• Connecticut	• Alabama
• California	• Michigan	• Maryland	• Arkansas
• Colorado	• Minnesota	• Massachusetts	• Florida
• Hawaii	• Missouri	• New Jersey	• Georgia
• Nevada	• Ohio	• New York	• Louisiana
• Texas	• Wisconsin	• Pennsylvania	• Mississippi
		• Washington DC	• North Carolina
			• South Carolina
			• Tennessee
			• Virginia

How do you sign up?

First, you want to search NACA.com and look up where a NACA office is located in relation to where you live within one of the states listed above. There is a bi-weekly class held for four hours on Saturdays at a participating NACA location where they will explain the NACA process. You must partake in an Intake Appointment with a Mortgage Counselor either over the phone or in person, during which you will discuss your payment history, income stability and determine readiness of homeownership. The next steps in your home buying process and becoming NACA qualified are also a part of the discussion.

Pros:

The program allots you the ability to purchase a single-family home, condo, townhouse or multi-unit property with little or no money down, no closing costs and no mortgage insurance (PMI). The interest rate is also lower than the national average, which means that it will cost less to finance the property than ordinarily. The fact that the program is a normal conventional loan with the ability to do 15yr or 30yr financing and that the loan is financed through one of the nation's largest lending institutions, Bank of America, are also pros of going through this program.

Cons:

You will have 100% financing with this program if you choose to put 0% down, which does mean that your monthly mortgage payment will be higher in relation. Going through the process of purchasing a home can be a year long process if all documentation is not submitted properly and on time. Also note that if your household makes a combined total income of 6-figures or greater, you will be considered a non-priority member, which means that you will have to search for a home within a low to moderate-income tract to be considered for the program.

CalHFA

What is CalHFA?

CalHFA, pronounced Cal-Ha-Fa, is a first time homebuyer down payment assistance program. CalHFA is a conventional loan program that does require mortgage insurance (PMI) but includes a fixed-rate interest rate and a 30yr-term loan.

Who is eligible?

First time homebuyers who complete the homebuyer education counseling through CalHFA and obtain a certificate of completion through an eligible homebuyer counseling organization. The course is provided in-person, face-to-face, through Neighborhood Works or a HUD-Approved Housing Counseling Agency; an online course for a set fee, can also be taken on your own accord.

One must meet the CalHFA income limits for this program, the sale price cannot exceed the CalHFA sales price limit and it must be an owner-occupied single-family home, one-unit residence including condo's/PUD's and manufactured homes are permitted. There is also a five acre max on the size of the property.

How do you apply?

You must find a CalHFA approved lender or find the lender that you would like to use and inquire if they offer the CalHFA program. You can find all of this information from calhfa.ca.gov.

Pros:

The program affords you the ability to receive up to 5% down payment (assistance towards the purchase price of your home which will help you get into your property without exhausting all of your funds.

HOME BUYING ON A BUDGET

Cons:

The program is not a grant, meaning that it has to be paid back with interest at the end of the loan terms (15yr or 30yr), when the property is sold or if you choose to refinance. The goal of the program is to have funds circulate. If you purchase a home using funds and do not pay them back, then they are essentially not available for another person or family to use. It's basically operating using the ideology of paying it forward.

Live in Los Angeles County?

HOP:

HOP, which stands for Home Ownership Program, is a loan that provides down payment and/or closing cost assistance up to $75,000 or 20% of the purchase price, whichever is less. The HOP loan is secured with a second Deed of Trust and Promissory Note. What does that mean? That means that you will have two loans instead of one; one that you pay back monthly via your mortgage, the other, the HOP loan is paid back if you sell the property secured with HOP loan funds, if the property has a transfer of ownership or is no longer owner-occupied. HOP loans are 0% interest deferred loans, so you pay back the exact amount of the loan that you borrow.

How can you qualify?

You must be a first-time homebuyer, which means that you must have not owned a home in the last three years, and the home you're looking to own must be owner-occupied. The annual income cannot exceed 80% of the median income for Los Angeles County based upon family size. You must contact one of the approved HOP participating lenders to be pre-qualified by visiting: https://wwwa.lacda.org/for-homeowners/homebuyer/home-ownership-program for a list of participating lenders. It is there that you can inquire with a participating lender what the current income requirements in order to qualify for the program are as well as eligible home prices are.

HOME BUYING ON A BUDGET

Eligible properties are single-family homes and attached or detached condominiums located in unincorporated areas of Los Angeles County and participating cities. You can find this information by visiting:

https://wwwa.lacda.org/for-homeowners/homebuyer/home-ownership-program.

First-time buyers must complete an 8-hour education in home ownership from an approved U.S. Department of Housing & Urban Development (HUD) counseling agency. Please visit www.hud.gov and follow the directions mentioned earlier to find one of the following agencies.

Pros:

If you qualify for the HOP loan, you can potentially qualify for a large down payment assistance which can not only help out with the down payment and closing costs, but can place you in a much higher loan qualifying amount by as much as $75,000.

Cons:

The HOP program is a loan, which means that it will have to be paid back. The other downfall to the HOP program is that it is another program that has a set amount of funds during varying times throughout the year. Funds are accessible based on availability, and you are not aware of the availability of the funds until you have an accepted offer on a property.

HOME BUYING ON A BUDGET

What are the home buying steps?

1. Pre-qualification

When you are in the market to purchase a home, there are a few steps prior to you receiving the keys. One of the very first steps that you can take when you are considering buying a home is to be pre-qualified. While its always a good idea to do research on the market that you plan on residing by attending open houses or using good old Google to not only understand the neighborhood but to get an idea of where the housing market is, a pre-qualification gives you an idea of how much of a loan you'll likely qualify for. It involves supplying a bank or lender with your overall financial picture, including your debt, income, and assets. The lender reviews all of this information and provides you with an estimate of how much you may be able to borrow for a home loan. This step is quick, typically taking within one to three days. It can be done over the phone or online and typically involves no costs. With that said, the pre-qualification is simply an estimate on what you can qualify for based on the information that you have provided, but does NOT take an in-depth analysis at your ability to purchase a home. Since it is based solely on the information that you provide, it doesn't mean very much if the information that you provide is inaccurate.

The pre-qualification step allows you to discuss, with a lender, the needs that you may have regarding your mortgage. Essentially, a pre-qualification, or "pre-qual" as it is often called, is the amount for which you might expect to be approved. Once you have been pre-qualified, you will have a better idea of how much you can spend on a home. While you can put in an offer on a home with a pre-qualification letter, a pre-approved buyer does carry more weight as they have been through a more thorough investigation for the home loan process.

2. Pre-approval

Getting pre-approved is the next step and has much more involved than a pre-qualification. In order to be pre-approved, you must complete a mortgage application while providing the lender with all of the necessary documentation to perform an extensive

HOME BUYING ON A BUDGET

background on your financials as well as your current credit rating. The lender will approve you for a specified amount after reviewing your finances and as a result, you will have a much better indication of the interest rate that you'll be charged as the interest rate that you receive is often based upon your credit score. In some instances, you may be able to lock in your interest rate during your pre-approval time period. Often times, a pre-approval will last anywhere from 30 to 90 days, so if you do not get an accepted offer on a home within that time frame, you will have to be reevaluated again by your lender; this could affect how much you qualify for since things such as interest rates fluctuate daily. You are sometimes charged a fee for a pre-approval by a lender, which can amount to a few hundred dollars. When a lender does an analysis on your background in order to decipher if you will qualify for a loan, they will take a look at your two-year work history, credit score based upon your credit report, your assets and liabilities as well as your debt.

Let's pause here for a second to explain one of the most important aspects of the home buying process; credit score. When a lender runs your credit report, there are three credit reporting bureaus: Equifax, Transunion and Experian. Credit score, closely related to FICO score, is defined as a number assigned to a person that indicates to lenders their capability to repay a loan. A Credit score is like the grade that's given to your credit report and can range anywhere from 300 to 850. When you are provided with only one credit score, this is typically your highest credit score of the three credit bureaus, but a lender does not use the highest score. They will use the middle score of the three, essentially the average. In order to gain access to your credit score, you will often have to pay, whether one time or via a monthly fee. But if you're thinking of purchasing a home, it's best that you are well aware of this information. If you're not sure if you have any negative items reported on your credit report that could ultimately affect your score, it is best to pull your credit report every year, which you can do for free via annualcreditreport.com. Within this report, you will see if there has been any suspicious activity that has been reported on your credit. This should be done annually, whether you are in the home buying process or not.

What affects your credit? Payment history, credit utilization, length of credit history, new credit and credit mix. Payment history comprises 35% of your total credit score and is the most important factor in calculating one's credit score. One of the best ways for borrowers to improve their credit score is by making consistent timely payments. Things such as late payments and delinquencies will negatively affect your credit score, but note that late payments are not reported on your credit report until after 30 days; a payment due on the 1stbut you paid it late on the 21stwill not be reported to credit bureaus mentioned earlier because the payment was less than 30 days late.

Credit utilization, the percentage of available credit that has been borrowed, makes up less than 30% of your total credit score. Your credit score will be negatively affected by maxed out credit cards or credit cards with balances very close to their credit limit. By maintaining a credit balance at or below 30%, you will help improve your credit score. If your credit limit is $1,000, you'll want to have a maximum usage of $300 on the credit card.

Length of credit history is about 15% of your total credit score and has to do with the length of time each account has been open and the length of time since the account's most recent action. A longer credit history provides more information and offers a better picture of long-term financial behavior. It is also worth noting that if you simply do not use credit, there can be no credit history which will negatively affect your credit score.

New Credit, the act of opening up a new line of credit, accounts for only about 10% of your credit. However, opening up multiple lines of credit could suggest that you are in financial trouble, as it is seen as you needing significant access to lots of credit.

Last but not least, Credit Mix is the variety of credit that you have open. When you repay a combination of revolving credit – such as credit cards – and installment loans, such as mortgages and student loans, the following indicates that the borrower can handle all sorts of credit and generally represent less risk for lenders.

Why is credit SO important when purchasing a home? Well, essentially, the worse your credit score, the more you'll likely have to pay to borrow money. To give you an example, I had a client who's credit score was 677 but because they did not have a credit score of 680, the lender charged them an extra .25% on their interest rate. Doesn't sound like much until you realize that this additional

HOME BUYING ON A BUDGET

quarter of a % was going to cost my client an extra $20,000 throughout the duration of the loan.

Lets get back to the advantages of getting a pre-qualification and pre-approval. The advantages of getting a pre-qualification prior to a pre-approval is that you'll have an idea of how much of a loan a lender will qualify you for. Therefore you'll have an idea on how much you can purchase a home for, thus allowing you to decipher if you feel that you're ready to move forward with the home buying process or not. If you don't qualify for the amount of home that you want to purchase, you can go back to the drawing board and save more money, hustle to have more income or work towards getting your credit score up, or all three. My personal opinion is that if you qualify for something, anything at all, while it may not be your dream home, you can use that piece of property as leverage to get the property that you truly want.

There was a story that I once heard of this couple who had a dream of living in Cerritos, Ca. If you aren't aware of where that is, it's a city located in southern California that is sought after because of its suburban setting, low crime rate, along with one of the best school districts in the state; about 25 minutes outside of downtown Los Angeles. The couple couldn't afford to live in Cerritos yet, so instead of working their tails off to save the down on a home in Cerritos, Ca they purchased a home within their budget in Compton, Ca. I'm not sure if you have heard of the city of Compton, Ca but many have a bad perception of it due to the "war on drugs" era and the 1992 LA riots which left much of the city in shambles due to civil unrest. The city today is making a huge turnaround and is a haven for many investors. The point of the story is that the couple purchased a home in Compton, Ca and within a few years, sold that home and purchased one in their desired neighborhood of Cerritos, Ca. They used the equity from their home in Compton towards the down on the home in Cerritos by leveraging their asset.

By owning what you can afford now and then using that money to purchase what you want later, you not only invest in real estate which affords you the ability to stop paying towards someone else's mortgage, but you add to your net worth all while putting a cap on your "rent" amount as your monthly mortgage is set (with respect to taxes and insurance). To give you an example, I put down $5,000 on my property because of the homebuyer program that I went through, refinancing, or selling my property and use that money to put 20% down on a small house, thus eliminating mortgage insurance or PMI. which today has afforded me over $100,000 in equity. I could easily take that equity amount, whether a portion of it through I live in a 1 bedroom 1 bathroom condo that has afforded me that opportunity within just 5 years.

If you decide to put off the purchasing property until you are within reach of your desired home and have decided to save towards a down payment instead, you'll also want to insure that you are saving towards a down payment in the future. What do I mean by that? Well, if homes are worth $484,000 (using the national average this year), that means in order to put a down payment of 20%, you will need to have $96,800 right now, which does not include the cost of the loan (typically anywhere from 1-2% of the loan amount) nor the closing costs which vary from 2-5% of the loan amount. What if you don't have $96,800 right now, but can get there in lets say a few years time? The average home value increases by 3-5% a year depending on the location of the home, so in three years, when you plan on having the $96,800, it may now have increased to you needing a down as high as $101,900. While this is true for any down payment amount whether you plan on putting a down payment of 3% or 20%, you can be playing catch up while saving if you do not account for the increase year over year in home values.

3. Purchase Offer Letter

Back to the home buying steps. Once you have been pre-qualified or pre-approved and are satisfied with the amount that you have been qualified or approved for, you are able to not only officially go house hunting, but are able to put in an offer on a home. An offer letter, also known as a purchase offer and purchase agreement, is a written contract with all of the terms that you plan on purchasing the property under. There are many different ways in which your offer can vary from another; the first one being price. You can choose to put in the offer amount at the sales price of the property, above, or below the sales price, depending on your negotiating power or how much you feel the house is worth to you in its current condition.

Within your offer, you can negotiate on anything from wanting to keep the furniture and/or appliances, asking for the seller to cover your closing costs and/or home warranty, to things such as inspection, loan and appraisal time periods, to length of time you expect that you can close the deal. Once you submit your offer, the seller will accept, reject or counter your offer. If your offer is accepted, congratulations. Once the seller signs and returns your purchase offer, you are under contract and one step closer to closing on that property. If your offer is rejected, you will either have to resubmit another offer to the same property with terms more favorable to the sellers liking or submit an offer on a different property. If your offer letter is countered, you have to decipher where your negotiating power is. If you have a multiple counter situation and you want the property badly, you'll likely have to come in higher than the original price of the home, sometimes by a few thousand dollars and sometimes by several; this will all depend on how badly you like or want the property.

4. Accepted Purchase Offer

Once you receive an accepted offer, you will enter into a contract where the closing process has begun. All parties involved in a transaction – the buyer, seller, their agents, the lender, title or escrow agent, and possibly the buyer and seller's attorneys – begin the process with the understanding that the purchase agreement is final. Although, the purchase agreement can be amended to reflect last-minute contingencies or negotiations such as a problem discovered during a home inspection without sabotaging a deal. At this point, you will place part of your down payment, also known as EMD or Earnest Money Deposit, into an escrow account. This amount ranges anywhere from 1-3% of the agreed upon purchase price of the home. The higher your EMD amount, the more serious of a buyer you look to the seller. Some markets do not require an escrow account, so you'll want to consult with your real estate agent far ahead of time to ensure that you have enough liquid funds in place to clear the deposit.

5. Home Inspection

A few days after you have entered into a contract, you will schedule a home inspection with a professional inspector. The home inspection consists of a certified inspector coming out to check the home for any potential dangers that are within the home for major issues that may cause you to rethink purchasing that piece of property. The purpose of a home inspection is to look for major and minor defects ranging from structural problems, nonworking appliances and aspects of the home that may violate local building codes.

After an inspector is done, you will receive an inspection report on the property, typically within 24-48 hours of the inspection, showing you their findings. Some of the items within the report are simply suggestions that the inspector recommends be completed while others are often requirements for a traditional lender to finance the property. Once you have received this report, it is your choice to accept all findings, or request that the seller fix some or all of the items listed by the inspector. The seller may act in good faith and fix all or most of the items that you request or they may decide not to fix anything at all.

If for some reason you and the seller cannot come to an agreement on the requested repairs, then you have every right to back out of the deal and get your EMD back as long as you are acting within a timely manner. It is your job as the buyer to ensure that the inspection, the inspection report, and the requested repairs be submitted to the seller within the agreed upon inspection contingency time frame, or run the risk of losing your EMD.

Many lenders require a home inspection as a condition of the loan, but if yours does not, there is little downside to getting a thorough look at the home you're about to buy. The standard inspection cost range anywhere from $300 to $500 which the buyer typically pays and is based upon the size of the property. This will seem like a barging if the inspection uncovers a major problem with the property that needs to be fixed prior to closing.

6. Appraisal

An appraisal is the valuation of a property and/or land completed by an appraiser who determines the market value of the property. Lenders protect their investment, or at least reduce their likelihood for losses by commissioning an appraisal at some time prior to closing. The buyer, on or before the appraisal date or on the closing date, generally pays for the appraisal fee.

If the appraiser determines that the value of the home you want to purchase is at least as much as you agreed to pay for it or greater, there is no need to worry. However, if the appraisal comes in low – below the accepted purchase price – the lender will only agree to finance an amount equal to the appraised value. A low appraisal usually requires the buyer and seller to renegotiate the purchase price and amend the purchase agreement, potentially delaying the deal.

7. Loan Approval

Your loan approval typically comes through towards the end of the closing process as it can take a month or longer to underwrite. The underwriting process is an analysis of your qualifications in being approved for a loan. This is the last major piece of the puzzle that needs to fall into place for your closing to proceed as scheduled.

8. Closing

After the inspection and appraisal have been completed and your lender has approved your loan, you will receive the closing notice – time, date, participating agents (buyer's and seller's) and location of closing. You will also receive the closing disclosure at least three days prior to the closing date, which is a plain-estimate document that outlines all of your actual financial obligations related to the transaction – your actual closing costs, ongoing tax obligation, and a breakdown of your mortgage loan. A final walk-through is executed as well, normally within 24 hours of the scheduled closing time. On closing day, the house that you've agreed to buy proudly becomes yours and dancing your way through the front door can commence.

HOME BUYING ON A BUDGET

I'm ready to buy a home now. What do I do?

The most important thing when it comes to purchasing a home is to make sure that you have suitable credit and some savings. Your credit score is a measure of how likely you are to pay back your debts. If you have bad credit, the bank will consider an investment in you a risk, thus potentially offering you a subprime loan; a loan with higher than average interest rates to help offset the likelihood that you will default thus charging you more and ultimately resulting in you qualifying for a lower loan amount. If you do not have "good" credit you can still purchase a home and not necessarily through a subprime loan.

You can also get an FHA loan which will take a credit score as low as 580 in order to qualify for the 3.5% down payment amount. Have a credit amount lower than 580? You can still qualify for an FHA loan, but you will likely be required to put as much as 10% down on a property. This isn't necessarily a bad thing, considering you can always get an FHA home loan and refinance out once your credit is better a few years later. The most important thing is to get the property when it is least expensive which is more than likely today as opposed to tomorrow.

The reason why realtors always say that its always a good time to purchase is because it's true. Purchasing a home is an investment. You may gain some equity in a few years, but sit on a property for 20 or 30 years in any part of the United States and you're almost certainly guaranteed a hefty return on your initial investment, whether you purchase in a "good" neighborhood or not.

I put good in quotes there because a lot of people use the excuse that they cannot purchase when what they really mean is that they cannot afford to purchase where they want to live. If you live in the "hood" just remember that a lot of "hood" neighborhoods have become gentrified which is seen as a bad thing when you rent, as many who live there are typically priced out. But what if you owned in one of those gentrifying "hoods"? You may not be as bothered once you have your return on investment increase drastically as what was once undesirable is now sought after. Gentrification can only be a thing when those who are being pushed out do not own within the gentrifying neighborhood.

HOME BUYING ON A BUDGET

Stay encouraged

There are two lessons within this book that I want you to take with you, whether you are able to use one of the programs listed above or not:

1) Get in where you fit in

The day before attending an open house in Los Angeles, around the corner from the University of Southern California (USC), one of California's most prestigious private learning institutions, I went door-knocking to inform the neighbors. There was one man in particular whose house I knocked on that resonated with me. I almost passed the home due to the condition as it looked as though it was in the process of a complete gut or that it had been completely abandoned. He spoke to me about how he purchased that home in 1976 or 1977 and that back then, he purchased it for $60,000. If you are unaware of the neighborhood directly surrounding USC, you are not aware that it was considered very unsafe over there until recent years. He expressed to me that directly across the street, the police showed up on a weekly basis, that the building had several known drug users, gang bangers and countless incidents one would consider 'unsafe'.

I asked him why this neighborhood during that time, especially considering the safety of the neighborhood and he expressed to me that that was all that he could afford at that time. When arriving here in the '70s from the Philippines, the man had two choices; to rent in a much "better" neighborhood, or to purchase in a neighborhood within his means that was a lot less desirable. By choosing the latter, he has seen a tremendous increase in not only his home's value but also his net worth, as this home could easily sell for over $1,000,000 in its current condition. The man didn't focus on where he couldn't buy but instead focused on where he could.

2) Stay persistent

Understand that a lending institution does not want to willingly give funds away let alone the government. The programs are there if you find them. You will need to be in constant communication with your lender to ensure that they have all the necessary paperwork in place in order to provide these funds to you. This also means that you need to be active in ensuring that all paperwork that you need to provide to your lender is provided to them in a timely manner. This could be what makes the difference between you getting a grant approval or assistance program or not.

It took me almost a month to get my pre-qualification letter. For some people, that would have discouraged them and left them without the first time homebuyer funds. You are in control of your own destiny, so if you give up or don't believe that you can do something, you've already lost. Make sure that before jumping into any program that you are well aware of what the program terms are from day one of the loan until the loan is paid off, you sell the property, or worse, you find yourself in foreclosure.

Make sure that you ask these few simple questions to help ensure that you're not getting into an unfavorable loan:

·Is this a conventional loan?

·Is this a fixed rate loan or adjustable?

·Do you provide down payment or closing cost assistance programs?

·If so, do the assistance programs provided require repayment?

·Is there a pre-payment penalty?

·Is the APR based upon the prime rate or do you offer APR rates lower than the national average?

·How long are the terms of this loan? 15yo? 30yo or 20yo?

·What is the minimum down payment?

·What is the average % cost for closing costs?

·What is the cost of the loan? What % of the loan amount?

·Do you provide a buy-down and how much does it cost per point (percentage point) to buy down the loan? How low can I buy down the loan APR %?

HOME BUYING ON A BUDGET

Although these aren't exhaustive in keeping you from getting into a possible bad loan, having these questions answered can help you understand what you are getting yourself into. Remember, do not have a lender run your credit until you understand the terms of the loan and are comfortable with using that lending institution. Each time your credit is run, your credit score is lowered as a result, so you want to avoid this action until you are ready.

Once you have figured out your lending, you want to find a good realtor. Where do I find that? Well, there are several places to find a great realtor. A few places are:

·Referral through friends or family

·Realtor.com

·Asking co-workers

·Or contact the author of this book

Your best bet is to interview a few realtors. When I first started my house search, I remember finding an agent who I sat down and spoke with along with my mom, and at the end of our conversation, he handed me a buyers agreement to sign. Sounds like a harmless act, which it is, until I realized that for a year, I would have had to either use him as my agent or ask someone else to cut their fee, as he would get a percentage of anything that I purchased within the time frame of the contract. Ultimately, I could "fire" him or get out of a contract, but that could have resulted in a lot of fighting and potentially a legal battle if he decided that he did not want to honor my request.

Fast forward a few months, right before I got pre-qualified, I wanted to see a condo in Long Beach that I believe this agent had a tie to somehow; likely her brokerage was the listing office. We went around looking at several properties as I waited for my pre-qualification letter and I notified her that I wanted to put in an offer on a particular property out of the ones that we had viewed. The property had previously had litigation due to some poorly performed construction work and she didn't feel comfortable putting in the offer on my behalf, even though the property was cleared by the fire department and could now receive financing.

HOME BUYING ON A BUDGET

At that time, properties flew off of the market, so if you didn't put in an offer and inform the listing agent of your plans to do so, you were always too late. This property was listed for only $160,000 with a fireplace, two balconies, subterranean parking and guest parking, as well as a water feature that flowed through the complex. After going back and forth with this agent, she finally put in an offer for me upon which we found out that an offer had already been accepted and that the property was no longer available. This happened on another property as well, and ultimately, she had to go.

After firing this agent, my mom and I then found Crystal West who now happens to be my broker. To say that she was exactly what we needed is an understatement. She was aggressive enough for such a difficult and hot market, but not pushy to the point where I felt that I was being forced to buy anything. Within a month of putting in offers and having my offer rejected on many occasions due to stiff competition and likely a soft offer letter due to not having a lot of money, my offer was accepted.

Although I didn't get everything that I wanted, I got everything that I needed and then some. I went where I fit and focused on investing in a property that was realistic to my budget. When I looked for my property, I was realistic, I didn't focus on not being able to purchase in downtown Los Angeles, one of the hottest areas to live in Los Angeles County for Millennials. I realized that I qualified for only so much and that if I was going to purchase somewhere, it had to be an up and coming neighborhood, not an area that was extremely popular already.

The neighborhood in which I decided to purchase is considered an area that is being gentrified, even to this day. Think gentrification is a bad thing? Try owning your property and see if it changes your mind. There were countless incidences with homeless people and corner store robberies. I had many friends and colleagues who questioned why I would have purchased a property in this particular neighborhood. By doing so, it paid off as five years later, I am sitting on equity of over $100,000; that silent second I mentioned earlier that goes away after living in the property for five years is now gone and is now straight equity. This may not be as much as the man who lives near USC at $1,000,000 yet, but who knows; in 40 years, I may be there because I pay towards my own mortgage and not someone else's.

HOME BUYING ON A BUDGET

Benefits of Homeownership

Homeownership has always been a staple in the American Dream and considered a gateway to the middle class. In recent years, many families have chosen to find domestic delight without paying a mortgage. What they're missing are the big benefits of homeownership that just can't be replaced by renting. Research shows that owning your own home has distinct advantages over renting, especially when it comes to building your net worth and providing a stable environment for your family. If you're debating whether to rent or buy your next home, here is a list of 8 reasons why owning your own home is better than renting:

1. Its cheaper than renting

Although buying a house is more expensive than renting in the beginning, it can actually be cheaper than renting in the long run. According to Trulia.com, a real estate website owned by Zillow, homeownership is 38% cheaper on average than renting at the national level. They did a comparison of the costs of homeownership - maintenance, taxes, and insurance - to the total costs of renting for the same time period; those calculations based upon the traditional 20% down, 30-year fixed-rate mortgaged.

They attribute the drastic difference to the rising costs of rent, which is not to say that buying a home isn't expensive, but the fact is by paying more upfront on your own home, you can actually save money in the long run.

2. You can build equity

One of the most significant benefits of homeownership is building equity - the difference between the market value of your home and the amount that you still owe. If you purchase a property at $300,000 and its appraised value is currently at $325,000 but you have a loan on the property at $270,000, then you have $55,000 in equity. Each time your home increases in value, your equity increases even though the amount that you owe doesn't. A study by Merrill Lynch found that homeowners under the age of 35 on average have equity valued at around $53,000 but homeowners over the age of 65 have on average $212,000 in equity. Instead of your money disappearing into your landlord's pockets, you'll be paying into something that is yours that can become more valuable over time.

3. Homeownership increases your net worth

Homeownership is an effective way to build one's net worth and has been the most tried and true method of doing so. You can calculate your net worth by subtracting your liabilities from your assets: investments, savings accounts, retirement funds, home equity, and other valuables. It is estimated that 67% of the average American's net worth is attributed to housing. While there are most certainly many different ways to invest your money, a house can serve as a way to build your net worth.

4. Your house can increase in value over time

Let's be frank — many learned the hard way in 2008 that property doesn't always appreciate in value over time, but guess what; many experts believe that the worst is behind us. Your home's value may increase each year that you own it. Zillow economist Stan Humphries estimates that the average house appreciates in value around 3.5% each year, but some areas experience greater increases.

What are the signs that tell in which area your home will likely increase in value? The property being located next to good schools, "up-and-coming neighborhoods", local employment, and even its proximity to Starbucks are all signs that your home could end up being worth more than the buying price.

5. Tax Deductions

While owning a home comes with great pride, it also comes with many responsibilities as well as expenses; the upside to the expenses, though, is that in some cases, they can be tax deductible. Potential deductions paid monthly on the mortgage on your property include interest, property taxes and private mortgage insurance premiums. As a homeowner, you have expenses on things like maintenance and repairs, but a luxury that you have that a renter does not is being able to deduct a portion of your monthly housing expenses on your taxes.